God of Healing

Susan Hardwick

First published in 1998 by
KEVIN MAYHEW LTD
Rattlesden
Bury St Edmunds
Suffolk IP30 0SZ

© 1998 Susan Hardwick

The right of Susan Hardwick to be identified as the author of this work has been asserted by her in accordance with the Copyright, Designs and Patents Act 1988.

All rights reserved. No part of this publication may be reproduced, stored in a retrieval system, or transmitted, in any form or by any means, electronic, mechanical, photocopying, recording or otherwise, without the prior written permission of the publisher.

ISBN 1 84003 170 0
Catalogue No 1500179

0 1 2 3 4 5 6 7 8 9

Cover design by Jaquetta Sergeant
Edited by Katherine Laidler
Typesetting by Louise Selfe
Printed and bound in Great Britain

CONTENTS

THE FIRST WORD	5
PRAYERS	7
DARK: SUFFERING	7
Grasp my cross, Lord	7
It's hard to keep the suffering in	8
I cry out to you, God	8
Dear God, why?	9
The day will dawn for me – won't it?	10
DAWN: HEALING	10
You come in many guises	10
The yearned-for sunrise	12
DAY: WHOLENESS	13
You have transformed my suffering	13
From the Cross to Resurrection	14
Your vision of wholeness	15
Make me now a source of healing to others	16
REFLECTIONS	
A TALE OF HEALING AND WHOLENESS	17
REFLECTION	20

WORDS FROM SCRIPTURE	27
The Old Testament	27
The New Testament	29
THE LAST WORD	31

ACKNOWLEDGEMENTS

Bible quotations are taken from:

– The Holy Bible, *New International Version*, © Copyright 1973, 1978, 1984 by International Bible Society, published by Hodder and Stoughton Ltd. All rights reserved. 'NIV' is a registered trademark of International Bible Society. UK trademark number 1448790.

– *The New Jerusalem Bible* published and © Copyright 1985 by Darton Longman and Todd Ltd and Doubleday and Co Inc. and used by permission of the publisher.

– *The Message* © Copyright by Eugene H. Peterson, 1993, 1994, 1995, 1996, 1997. Used by permission of NavPress Publishing Group.

THE FIRST WORD

From darkness through the dawn to daylight, from our experiences of suffering through to wholeness, God's constancy, commitment and love never fail. We may not always recognise him, but he is there.

Using prayers, stories, reflections and Bible passages, this little book reflects on that truth.

Most of our opposite experiences are two sides of the same coin: one emphasises the other, as do darkness and light, night and day. Just as night and day are integral to the rhythm of Creation, so are our negative and positive experiences integral to our human condition.

The secret of joyful, fearless living, then, is to be as ready to embrace the one as the other, in confidence and trust and expectation that, when we are in the difficult, hard times, the dawn will finally break upon the night sky and dispel the darkness.

The title CROSS+WORDS reflects the truth that, through our prayer and Christ's Cross, we are linked to the healing touch of Jesus upon and within our lives.

SUSAN HARDWICK

PRAYERS

Don't fret or worry. Instead of worrying, pray. Let petitions and praises shape your worries into prayers, letting God know your concerns. Before you know it, a sense of God's wholeness, everything coming together for good, will come and settle you down. It's wonderful what happens when Christ displaces worry at the centre of your life.
Philippians 4:5b-7 (The Message)

DARK: SUFFERING

Grasp my cross, Lord

Body, mind and spirit
– there seems no part of me
that is not affected.
Jesus,
Healer,
from your suffering Cross
reach out and grasp mine.
Amen.

It's hard to keep the suffering in

There's a weariness
about continuous, gnawing pain
that wears away
at the strongest resolve
not to complain.
I don't want to sound self-pitying,
but it's so very hard
to keep all the suffering in,
and not to let on
how much it hurts.
Give me courage,
Lord,
not to despair.
And give me wisdom
to know how much,
and with whom,
I can and should share.
Amen.

I cry out to you, God

O God!
From the midst of my suffering,
from the bottom of my heart,

I cry out to you –
help me!
Amen.

Dear God, why?

Dear God,
why?
It seems so very unfair.
What *have* I done
to deserve this suffering?

I may not be perfect.
But at least I *try*
– yet still I end up
with all of this.

Why *do* bad things happen
to good people?
Why not to the bad ones, instead?

Help me to understand.
But, above all,
help me *not* to be bitter.
Amen.

The day will dawn for me – won't it?

Jesus –
'As surely as the day
follows the night, so the good follows the bad.'
I really do believe this for others.
In the midst of my present darkness,
help me to trust
that it will be so for me as well.
But, until that day dawns,
stay very close beside me.
May your presence,
your Cross,
remind me
that no suffering is for ever.
Amen.

Dawn: Healing

You come in many guises

Lord,
there is a loneliness
and an isolation in suffering
which strikes at the very heart

of the person concerned.
It's so hard to look outwards
when the pain is drawing you in.

And so I give you thanks
for those who have ministered to me
by their concern and their care;
by just being there
at my point of need.
Sometimes I have not recognised
your face and your presence
in them and in their actions,
and that you come to me
through them.

Give me the eyes
to see you everywhere,
in your many guises.
Give me a heart
full of gratitude,
reaching back out to you
as you reach out to me.
Thank you.
Amen.

The yearned-for sunrise

Jesus,
we are told that,
at the hour of your death,
night covered the land
– yet it was still only afternoon.
The darkness was a fitting symbol
of all of your suffering.

But neither the night
nor your pain,
lasted for ever.
Your faith and your trust
took you through
to the dawn.

And so it has been with me.
The yearned-for sunrise
is beginning to tinge the sky.
Now I can see
hope and healing
where before there seemed
only suffering and despair.

Throughout that long, dark night,
you were always close by.

Unseen, maybe,
but always present.
Only a hand-touch away.
Jesus, Saviour,
by your wounds
I am healed.
Amen.

Day: Wholeness

You have transformed my suffering

Most wondrous God,
you have taken my suffering,
and transformed it
into something totally other.
I was fragmented by weariness
and anguish and pain,
but you have drawn me together,
and made me whole again.
You are greatly to be praised!
Amen.

From the Cross to Resurrection

Jesus,
from Good Friday to Easter Day!
From the Cross to Resurrection!
Through your suffering
you have given infinite meaning
to suffering,
and planted your Cross firmly
in every place
where there is pain
of any kind.
And so it was for me.
In my darkness you gave me hope,
and carried me through
to this bright day.
Thank you!
Amen.

Your vision of wholeness

Sometimes, Lord,
just *sometimes*,
I get glimpses
of the possibilities
running through the whole
of your Creation.
Golden opportunities
which would be
ours to reach out for
and to grasp
if only we had the courage
so to do.

Then we would
'fly with eagle's wings,
run and not be weary':
visions of wholeness,
of realising the potential
that is within
each one of us.

So, Lord, I pray:
help me to become
your vision of me.
Amen.

Make me now a source of healing to others

Jesus,
you touch each of us
according to our need.
In your infinite wisdom,
you knew exactly
what was right for me
to make me whole once more.

Help me now to turn my attention
to others who suffer.
As you reached out to me,
so may I reach out to them.
May I be a source of healing
in my turn.
Amen.

REFLECTIONS

O God,
without you,
nothing makes sense.
Psalm 16:1b (The Message)

A TALE OF HEALING AND WHOLENESS

There was a knock at the vicarage door. It was evening, and there was an autumn chill in the air.

Wearily, the vicar opened the door. It had been a hard, long day, and he had only just sat down with his family.

In the porch stood a tall young man, who said he was homeless and please could the priest help him.

The man waited in the front garden, whilst the vicar phoned the local hostel for the homeless to see if there were any places.

When the vicar's wife realised what was happening, she went outside. 'Wouldn't you like to come in?' she asked the tall young man, who was admiring the flowers. He smiled his gratitude, came in and sat on a chair in the hallway.

'Would you like a cup of tea?'

'Why, *thank you*. That would be lovely.'

'A sandwich?'

'Thank you. But no.'

That was surprising. Rarely was food refused. The vicar's wife was used to all kinds of people turning up like this and for a variety of reasons. Some of the stories they told were so far-fetched they would have made good storylines for a book.

But this one was different. She could not quite define it. His manner, and style of talking, were only a part of it. There was something else. Subtle. Indefinable.

She popped her head round the door, whilst the kettle was boiling.

'Would you like anything else? A banana, perhaps? They're very nourishing.'

The tall young man laughed. It was a *beautiful* sound. Soft and low and full of delight, the like of which she had never heard before.

And his expression – it glowed with goodness and peace.

'Thank you! I should *love* a banana.'

The vicar's wife took her mug of tea into the hall, so she could keep the stranger company whilst he waited.

'Do you have many people like me come to your door seeking help?' he asked.

'Yes, quite a few. They come for a variety of reasons,' she replied.

But they are not like you, she thought. Who *are* you?

She was normally so socially competent, and could talk easily with people from all walks of life and situations. But this young man made her feel self-conscious and confused, as if he could see into her heart. As if he understood her very well indeed.

After a few more moments of conversation, the vicar came out of his study. 'I've fixed you up with a bed for the night. When you've finished your tea, I'll run you there in the car.'

The young man stood up. He was, indeed, very tall.

He turned to the woman. 'Thank you,' he said, softly. There was a world of meaning in the two words.

The woman felt his presence intensely. It was as if he had an aura about him. For some reason, she could not look up at him. His words had felt like a blessing, a benediction.

She stood at the door, and watched as the car turned into the road.

'Who *are* you?' she said again to herself. 'And where did you *really* come from?'

A few weeks later, when she was praying, she felt an aching longing to see Jesus – as he had really been and not as some imaginary picture. 'O Lord,' she prayed, 'how I envy those who were able to see you in your earthly life. To know you then, and what you looked like. How I *wish* it could have been me!'

Into her mind flooded a clear and vivid image of the tall young man who had called at their door seeking help.

And, with it, came an overwhelming sense of peace and healing and wholeness.

Reflection

The whole question of suffering is a huge one. Why there is suffering, and what purpose does it serve, are questions which have always haunted people, it seems. Many, many books have been written on the subject, and many more sermons preached.

Similarly, its sister subject of healing.

As some of our prayers at the beginning of this book indicate, there is the healing which we experience when we are relieved of our suffering either by the grace of God, or by the compassion of others, or both.

There is also the healing which we can bring to others by our own love and ministrations: more of that in a moment.

And then there is the healing which we can experience within ourselves at the same time as we give our love and support to others – as our story illustrates.

In his prose poem, 'Kristos', which he wrote in 1878, Turgenev portrays himself as a man dreaming that he is in a village church, together with the peasant congregation. Someone comes to stand beside him. Turgenev writes, 'I did not turn towards him, but immediately I felt that this man was Christ.' When, at last, he does turn towards him he sees a face 'like everyone's face . . . And the clothes on him like everyone else's . . . What sort of a Christ is this then? . . . Such an ordinary, ordinary man . . . Suddenly, I was afraid – and then I came to my senses. Only then did I realise that it is just such a face – a face like all men's faces – that is the face of Christ.'

> Continue to love each other like brothers,
> and remember always to welcome strangers,
> for by doing this,

some people have entertained angels
without knowing it.
Hebrews 13:1, 2 (NJB)

Jesus said,
'I tell you the truth,
whatever you did
for one of the least of these sisters or
brothers of mine,
you did for me.'
Matthew 25:40 (NIV, adapted)

Our tale of the stranger at the door and of healing and wholeness is really about meeting people at their point of need, as Jesus did – seeing ourselves as agents of the healing of others in our turn; seeing healing as the responsibility of each one of us, and not as the responsibility always of others.

It is *not*, of course, about letting people into your house inappropriately, for that would neither be safe nor wise. It *is*, however, about taking the opportunities that present themselves to reach out to those who suffer, and who are 'knocking on the door' of our hearts.

It is very easy to convince ourselves that all the suffering and all the pain in the world is someone else's problem.

One day it might be us on the outside, knocking on the door of other people's hearts, and begging for a response.

Jesus once told the story of the Good Samaritan (Luke 10:25f.) as an example of various responses to suffering.

Suffering comes in all sorts of shapes and forms.

It can be like water, seeping into every area of a person's life and every fibre of their body, and overwhelming every other feeling. It can give a sense of powerlessness and helplessness that there is nothing the sufferer can do to stop the suffering.

It can also feel so very lonely, for no one else can bear it for you.

Suffering is universal, so the problem of suffering, whether it be physical, mental, emotional or spiritual, affects us all.

Suffering makes people cry out, 'Why?'

Jesus also cried out 'Why?' and 'No!'; then set about changing things. The Gospels are accounts of his journeying through suffering, others' as well as his own, and how he worked tirelessly and at great personal cost to alleviate all types of suffering wherever he went.

In his earthly ministry Jesus was so alert to the suffering of others that he knew the difference between the press of the crowds and the touch on the hem of his garment by someone in need of his healing touch.

> Now, when Jesus returned,
> a crowd welcomed him,
> for they were all expecting him . . .
> As Jesus was on his way,
> the crowds almost crushed him.
> And a woman was there
> who had been subject to bleeding for
>   twelve years,
> but no one could heal her.
> She came up behind him
> and touched the edge of his cloak,
> and immediately the bleeding stopped.
> Jesus said, 'Someone touched me;
> I know that power has gone out from me.'
> *Luke 8:40-44, 46*

We hear, in John's account of Jesus' crucifixion:
> When the soldiers crucified Jesus,
> they took his clothes,
> dividing them into four shares,
> one for each of them,
> with the undergarment remaining.
> This garment was seamless,
> woven in one piece
> from top to bottom.
> *John 19:23 (NIV)*

His seamless garment, so finely woven that warp and weft could not be distinguished, is symbol of everything in this world finally woven together into the love of God.

Jesus' life, his death and his resurrection drawing together suffering, healing and wholeness.

Jesus, as both human and God in his earthly life, contained all divided worlds in himself. We are told he knew suffering and temptation in every respect, just as we do.

However, throughout his life, he drew together all the opposites in himself and let them converge, as he constantly reached out in the most authentic and appropriate way to each person according to his or her need.

Finally, on the Cross, he held together life and death itself.

As he opened wide his arms upon the Cross, he was welcoming everyone in need to come to him, to find healing and wholeness in him, and to be drawn through him to the Father.

We may not have Jesus' gifts of healing, nor his power – but we can watch, and pray, and stay alongside those who suffer.

We can work to improve those social conditions which cause or increase the suffering.

We can speak out against injustice, repression, neglect and torture: all things that cause untold amounts of suffering.

WORDS FROM SCRIPTURE

Jesus addressed the crowds, using this story:
'A farmer went out to sow his seed. Some of it fell on the road; it was trampled down and the birds ate it. Other seed fell in the gravel; it sprouted, but withered because it didn't have good roots. Other seed fell in the weeds; the weeds grew with it and strangled it. Other seed fell in rich earth and produced a bumper crop . . .

> This is the meaning of the parable:
> the seed is the Word of God.'
> *Luke 8:5-8, 11 (The Message)*

The Old Testament

God said,
'I have heard your prayer
and seen your tears;
I will heal you'.
2 Kings 20:5b (NIV)

Those who suffer
God delivers in their suffering;
he speaks to them
in their affliction.
Job 36:15 (NIV)

O Lord, heal me,
for my bones are in agony.
My soul is in anguish.
How long, O Lord, how long?
Psalm 6:2b-3 (NIV)

For God has not despised or disdained
the suffering of the afflicted one;
he has not hidden his face from him
but has listened
to his cry for help.
Psalm 22:24 (NIV)

O Lord, have mercy on me;
heal me,
for I have sinned against you.
Psalm 41:4 (NIV)

Heal me, O Lord, and I shall be healed;
save me and I shall be saved,
for you are the one I praise.
Jeremiah 17:14 (NIV)

'For you who revere my name',
says the Lord Almighty,
'the sun of righteousness will rise
with healing in its wings.'
Malachi 4:2a (NIV)

The New Testament

Jesus also drove out many demons,
but he would not let the demons speak
because they knew who he was.
Mark 1:34b (NIV)

Jesus then began to teach them
that the Son of Man must suffer many things
and be rejected . . . and that he must be killed
and after three days rise again.
Mark 8:31 (NIV)

The Roman centurion sent to Jesus to ask him
if he would heal his servant, saying,
'Lord . . . just say the word
and my servant will be healed.'
When those who had been sent returned,
they found the servant well.
Luke 7:7, 10 (NIV, adapted)

You know . . . how God anointed
Jesus of Nazareth
with the Holy Spirit and power,
and how he went around doing good and
   healing . . .
because God was with him.
Acts 10:37f. (NIV)

Suffering produces perseverance;
perseverance, character;
and character, hope.
Romans 5:3b, 4 (NIV)

There should be no division in the body
[of the community]
but its parts should have equal concern for
   each other.
If one part suffers, every part suffers with it.
1 Corinthians 12:25, 26a (NIV)

Pray for each other so that you may be healed.
James 5:16b (NIV)

By Jesus' wounds you have been healed.
1 Peter 2:24b (NIV)

THE LAST WORD

I am well on my way,
reaching out for Christ,
who has so wondrously reached out for
 me . . .
I've got my eye on the goal
where God is beckoning us onward –
 to Jesus.
I'm off and running,
and I'm not turning back.
So let's keep focused on that goal,
those of us who want everything God has
 for us.
If you have something else in mind,
something less than total commitment,
God will clear your blurred vision –
you'll see it yet!
Now that we're on the right track
let's stay on it.
Don't waver.
Stay on track,
steady in God.
Philippians 3:12-16; 4:1b (The Message)

Jesus said:
'You didn't choose me, remember;
I chose you,
and I put you in the world
to bear fruit,
fruit that won't spoil.'
John 15:16a (The Message)